The word "Pelican" and the depiction of a pelican are trademarks of Arcadia Publishing Company Inc. and are registered in the U.S. Patent and Trademark Office.

Library of Congress Cataloging-in-Publication Data

Names: Rust, Nancy, author. | Stubbs, Carol, author. | Nicol, Brock, illustrator.
Title: Andrew Higgins and the boats that landed victory in World War II / Nancy Rust, Carol Stubbs ; illustrated by Brock Nicol.
Description: New Orleans : Pelican Publishing, (2020) | Summary: "Andrew Higgins built boats that could 'crunch through driftwood, bounce over logs, climb a beach,' and 'wham up on a sloping concrete sea wall.' In World War II, that was exactly what was needed to get soldiers and Jeeps from the ocean to land. This biography for young readers traces the invention of the legendary Higgins boat—and the adventurous childhood of the remarkable man behind it"-- Provided by publisher.
Identifiers: LCCN 2019042412 | ISBN 9781455625277 (hardback) | ISBN 9781455625284 (ebook)
Subjects: LCSH: Higgins, Andrew, 1886-1952. | Landing craft--United States--Juvenile literature. | Boatbuilders--United States--Juvenile literature. | Landing craft--United States--Design and construction. | World War, 1939-1945--Amphibious operations--Juvenile literature.
Classification: LCC V895 .R87 2020 | DDC 623.825/6092 (B)--dc23
LC record available at https://lccn.loc.gov/2019042412

Printed in Malaysia

Published by Pelican Publishing
New Orleans, LA
www.pelicanpub.com

For our dads, Alfred Shearer and Robert Maeser, Jr., and all others who served in World War II and for all who supported our country during that time—N. R. and C. S.

Andrew liked challenges, and he loved boats, especially fast boats.

Andrew Higgins was born in 1886 in Columbus, Nebraska. He was the youngest of ten children. His father died when he was seven, and his mother moved the family to Omaha. His home was near a large lake.

Andrew built his first boat when he was twelve. He spotted a wrecked sailboat in the lake. He pulled the boat to shore and set to work.

He measured. He sawed. He leveled. He sanded and painted. He worked and worked and worked. At last, the boat was ready to sail. He named the boat *Patience,* because he had needed so much patience while he worked on it. Andrew expected *Patience* to zoom across the water. He was disappointed. *Patience* was way too slow.

Andrew decided to build a faster boat, one that would speed across ice. He built this boat in his basement and named her *Annie O,* to honor his mother. But *Annie O* was too big to take out the door—another challenge!

Andrew waited until his mother went shopping. After she left, he and his friends tore down part of the basement wall and took the boat out through the hole. They had put most of the wall back before his mother came home.

The speedy *Annie O* gave Andrew the excitement he wanted. School did not. It moved too slowly for him, so he quit. But he never stopped reading and learning how to do new things. He became a soldier. He drove a truck. He cut and loaded lumber. He became a farmer. He bought a lumber mill. But he was never satisfied.

& EXPORT CO.

He moved to the South. At first, he lived in Alabama. Then he moved to New Orleans. It was a city near water and trees. It was exactly what Andrew wanted! He opened a lumber business.

Cypress trees grew in the swamps near New Orleans. Cutting the trees was easy, but getting them to the lumber mill was hard. Boats hauled the trees out of the swamps. The shallow water caused problems. Sometimes boats got stuck on sandbars. Sometimes they bumped into logs. And they moved very, very slowly.

Andrew needed a better boat, so he began building boats. He looked for new design ideas. He examined the Cajun pirogue. It had a flat bottom. He studied a tunnel boat in Holland. He watched the way a blue whale moved in the water. He looked at the shape of a spoonbill. He copied the ramp of a Japanese landing boat. The lumber business slowed down. Andrew's main business became boatbuilding.

Andrew made better and better boats. He was proud of them. He said his boats could "crunch through driftwood, bounce over logs, climb a beach," and "wham up on a sloping concrete sea wall." More and more people wanted Andrew's boats.

Then World War II began. Andrew was making the best landing boats in the world. They were called Higgins boats. The boats were just what the Allies needed! They needed boats to carry the soldiers from the big ships to the shore. They needed boats to land tanks. They needed thousands and thousands of Higgins boats. And they needed them fast.

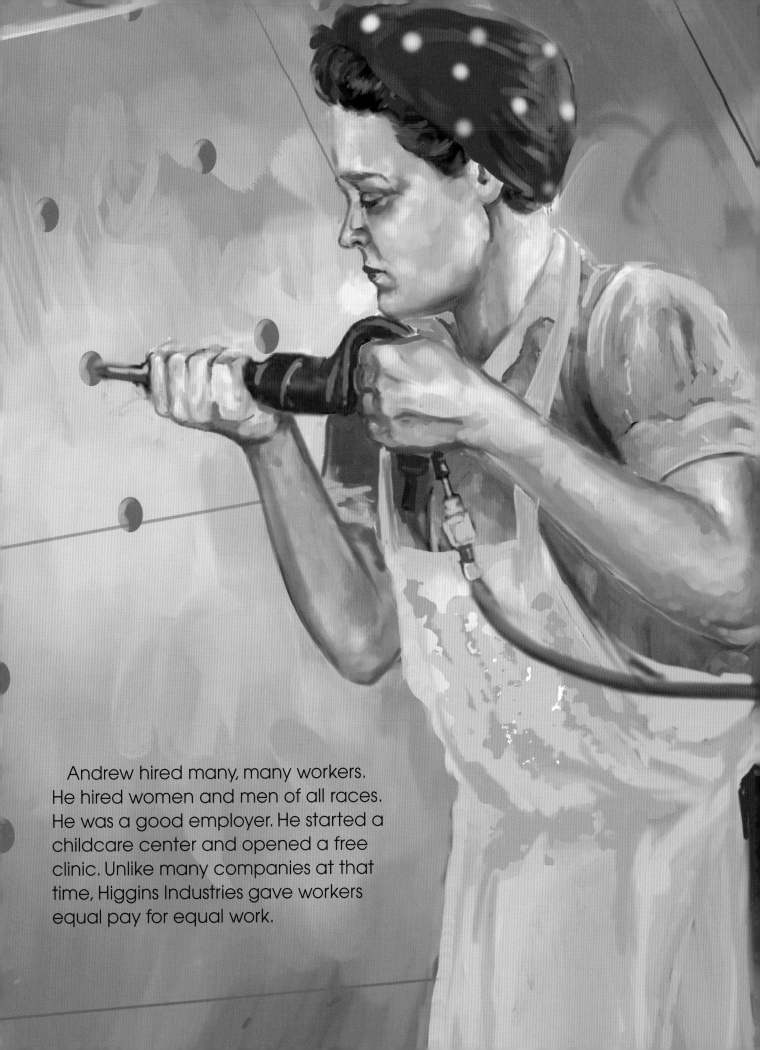

Andrew hired many, many workers. He hired women and men of all races. He was a good employer. He started a childcare center and opened a free clinic. Unlike many companies at that time, Higgins Industries gave workers equal pay for equal work.

Andrew found ways to build boats more quickly. His workers built boats on a second floor, so the boats could be lowered onto railroad cars. They assembled boats in a canal. Andrew even covered a city block with a canvas roof. He used it as a warehouse and workplace.

Higgins boats forever changed the way
wars were fought. The boats moved countless
soldiers and tons of equipment. They landed
on sandy shores and rocky coasts. They landed
on continents and islands. They landed on
beaches from the tropics to the arctic. Higgins
boats were a bridge from ship to shore for
hundreds of thousands of brave soldiers.

Years later, Pres. Dwight D. Eisenhower was asked about the war. He talked about Andrew. He said that the boy from Nebraska who loved boats was "the man who won the war."

Glossary

Allies. States or countries cooperating with each other for military purposes. In World War II, the Allied countries included the United States, France, Britain, China, Soviet Union, Canada, and Australia.

Cajun pirogue. A small, flat-bottomed boat that moves easily through shallow water.

cypress tree. An evergreen tree found in the swamps of Louisiana.

Dwight D. Eisenhower. Supreme commander of the Allied Forces during World War II and thirty-fourth president of the United States.

lumber mill. A factory that cuts logs into wooden boards for building.

spoonbill. A long-legged wading bird that has a long bill with a wide, flat tip.

swamps. Low lands covered with shallow water.

tunnel boat. A racing boat design that allows for a "tunnel" of air to flow between the water and the boat.

Author's Note

Dear Reader,

When we were your age, we didn't know about Andrew Higgins. We learned about him when we were adults and visited the National World War II Museum in New Orleans. We saw that President Eisenhower had said Andrew Higgins was "the man who won the war for us." He even earned a gold medal from Congress for his war efforts. Who was this man?

In researching Andrew Higgins, we found a boy who lost his father at a young age, a lively boy who had problems in school, a boy who had a big imagination, and a boy who liked a challenge. This boy grew into a bold man who never stopped searching for ways to make life better—not just for himself, but also for others. When he noticed that boats were getting stuck in the swamps near New Orleans, he built one for shallow water. When he started a company, he made sure the workers were treated fairly and compassionately. When he saw the world headed toward war, he designed boats that could land soldiers and equipment. When his country went to war and needed those boats, he opened factories to produce over twenty thousand landing craft, and he trained sailors and marines to use them. When the Allies landed at Normandy on D-Day, it was the Higgins boats that got them onto the beaches. From there, they moved through Europe to free millions of conquered people.

Sometimes all it takes is the imagination of one person to make the world a better place for a lot of people. That person could be you.

Important Dates

1886	Andrew Higgins is born in Columbus, Nebraska.
1893	Higgins family moves to Omaha, Nebraska.
1898	Andrew builds *Patience.*
1900	Andrew enrolls in Creighton Preparatory School.
1903	Andrew joins the Nebraska National Guard.
1906	Andrew moves to Alabama.
1908	October 16, Andrew marries Angele Colsson.
1910	Andrew and Angele move to New Orleans.
1916	A. J. Higgins Lumber and Export Company opens.
1923	Company changes focus from lumber to boatbuilding.
1926	The shallow-draft *Eureka* boat is developed.
1927	Andrew's boats gain recognition for performance during the Great Flood.
1930	September 26, Higgins Industries is incorporated.
1937	Higgins sells boats to U.S. Coast Guard and U.S. Army Corps of Engineers.
1938	May 5, Higgins Industries gets first contract from U.S. Navy.
1939	World War II begins with German invasion of Poland. United States is neutral.
1939	Higgins orders two shiploads of Philippine mahogany wood for boatbuilding.
1940	Higgins designs his first PT (patrol torpedo) boat.
1941	First Higgins boats with ramps are built.
1941	December 7, Japan bombs Pearl Harbor. December 8, United States declares war.
1942	March 9, U.S. Navy orders 508 landing craft.
1943	Higgins Industries has seven plants and employs more than twenty-five thousand workers.
1943	More than 90 percent of U.S. Navy's 14,072 vessels are Higgins designs.
1944	June 6, D-Day, more than one thousand Higgins boats ferry soldiers and vehicles to Normandy beaches.
1944	June 23, celebration in New Orleans for delivery of 10,000th Higgins boat to U.S. Navy.
1945	May 7, Germany surrenders. September 2, Japan surrenders. World War II ends.
1952	Andrew Higgins dies in New Orleans.
2001	Congress awards gold medals to the family of Andrew Higgins and the wartime employees of Higgins Industries.
2019	Andrew Higgins is inducted into the National Inventors Hall of Fame.